**Turbo**, the fast cane transporter, loved **racing across the farm**.

He always worked hard, but he never missed a chance to **zoom around the fields!**

One day, as **Turbo** was finishing his last load of the day, he noticed dark clouds gathering in the sky.

"**Looks like a storm is coming,**" he thought.

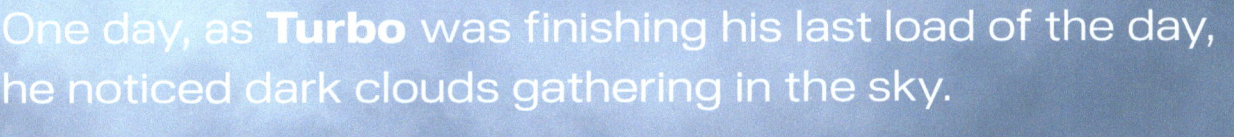

**Turbo** hurried to unload his cane at the siding, hoping to beat the rain.

But as he reached the bins, a **strong wind began to blow**.

"Whoa!" **Turbo** exclaimed, struggling to keep steady.

**The wind is getting stronger,** and the clouds are getting darker.

Just then, **Flash**, Turbo's twin brother, appeared beside him.

"We need to get back to the shed before the storm hits!" **Flash shouted**.

**Turbo** nodded, but just as they turned to leave, they heard a **loud crash echo through the fields**.

THAT WAS CLOSE!

A large branch had fallen onto the track right in front of **Libby**, the locomotive!

**Libby** was pulling a full load of cane to the Sugar Mill.

"Oh no!" said **Turbo**.

"**Libby** won't be able to get the cane to the Sugar Mill if that branch stays there!"

**Turbo** felt a raindrop hit his bonnet.

"We need to hurry!" he urged. "The rain is starting!"

Libby blew her whistle in encouragement.

"Come on, Turbo and Flash! We can do this together!"

With one last push from **Turbo**, **Flash**, and **Libby**, the branch finally rolled off the tracks.

"**We did it!**" Flash cheered.

Libby smiled in relief.

"Thank you, **Turbo** and **Flash**! Now I can get the cane to the Sugar Mill before the rain hits!"

The twins waved as **Libby** chugged away.

"**Now let's get back to the shed before the storm gets worse!**" Turbo said.

**Turbo** and **Flash** sped off, racing against the wind and rain.

The sky was now dark, and lightning struck in the distance.

"**That was close!**" Turbo said, shaking off the raindrops.

Flash nodded. "**Yeah, but we made it, and we helped Libby get to the Sugar Mill on time!**"

As the storm raged outside,
**Turbo** and **Flash** settled in, grateful to be safe and dry.

"**We make a great team,**" Turbo said.
Flash nodded in agreement.
"**Together, we can face any storm.**"

www.ingramcontent.com/pod-product-compliance
Lightning Source LLC
Chambersburg PA
CBHW041409160426
42811CB00106B/1561